SAGITTARIUS
HOROSCOPE 2015

Lisa lazuli

Lisa Lazuli is the author of the amazon bestseller

HOROSCOPE 2014: ASTROLOGY and NUMEROLOGY HOROSCOPES

ABOUT THE AUTHOR

Lisa Lazuli studied astrology with the Faculty of Astrological Studies in London.

She has practiced since 1999.

Lisa has been a regular guest on BBWM and BBC Shropshire talking about astrology and doing both horoscopes and live readings. She has also made guest appearances on Fox FM, BBC Cambridgeshire, BBC Northamptonshire, BBC Coventry and Warwickshire and US Internet Radio Shows including the Debra Clement Show.

Lisa wrote horoscopes for Asian Woman Magazine.

Now available in eBook and paperback:

TAURUS: Your Day, Your Decan, Your Sign *The most REVEALING book on The Bull yet.* Includes 2015 Predictions.

ARIES HOROSCOPE 2015

TAURUS HOROSCOPE 2015

GEMINI HOROSCOPE 2015

CANCER HOROSCOPE 2015

LEO HOROSCOPE 2015

VIRGO HOROSCOPE 2015

LIBRA HOROSCOPE 2015

SCORPIO HOROSCOPE 2015

Lisa Lazuli is also the author of

The mystery/thrillers:

A Sealed Fate

Holly Leaves

Next of Sin

<u>As well as:</u>

Delicious, Nutritious Recipes for the Time and Cash Strapped

Paleo Diet: Get Started, Get Motivated, Feel Great.

99 ACE Places to Promote Your Book

Pressure Cooking Reinvented.

FOREWARD

Dear Reader,

I hope my yearly horoscopes will provide you with some insightful guidance during what is a very tricky time astrologically speaking with the heavy planets i.e. Pluto and Uranus at loggerheads in cardinal signs and Neptune in Pisces calling us all to get in touch with our spiritual side.

I have a conversational style of writing, please excuse any grammatical errors, I write much as I would speak.

As the song goes, "Nobody said it was easy." I know the mass media pump-out shows us plenty about quick fix love, money, fame and success; however, life is a journey filled with challenges and obstacles designed to encourage us to find out what we are made of and who we really are.

Embrace the good and bad and enjoy what is your unique experience.

Be the hero in your own personal life movie and never hide your spotlight.

I must add that the best astrology insights are gained from a unique chart based on your time, date, year and place of birth.

If you would like your natal chart calculated for FREE, click here:

http://lisalazuli.com/2014/06/30/would-you-like-to-know-where-all-your-planets-are-free-natal-chart/

Please join me on facebook:

https://www.facebook.com/pages/Lisa-Lazuli-Astrologer/192000594298158?ref=hl

Contents

Overview 9

    JANUARY 2015..15

    FEBRAURY 2015..19

    MARCH 2015 23

    APRIL 2015 27

    MAY 2015...31

    JUNE 2015..35

    JULY 2015...37

    AUGUST 2015 41

    SEPTEMBER 2015...45

    OCTOBER 2015...49

    NOVEMBER 2015 53

    DECEMBER 2015 57

A year of ideas, of teaching and learning. 2015 is about molding concepts into plans and solutions. You are on track mentally, and you can understand the way your life works and how you can organize yourself better via your understanding of situations and people and the way you handle information. New places and new people are very much the theme in 2015; with you experiencing a range of different circumstances to what you usually encounter.

They say that to change your life you have to change your thinking, and this is very true this year – a new insight, a changed attitude or new information can transform your life direction. Like-wise a PMA (positive mental attitude) can be the key to success in 2015, what you envision, you materialize – do beware though as thinking about negative things can also result in them materializing.

Restless by nature, Sagittarians are very open to anything that broadens their mind or their perspective, and this year you are given ample opportunity to challenge yourself physically, spiritually and philosophically. This year your life is in flux, and you need to be flexible and adaptable – while it is not a year of major changes, it is one of constant smaller changes which can at times come out of the blue. 2015 is full of variety, and you should not cling to routines strictly – keep your options open and be ready to change course at any time. Go with the flow and embrace what comes along – use the year as a chance to loosen your boundaries and expand your mindsets.

This year you are fueled with enthusiasm and curiosity; indeed, this is a wonderful year for those who are studying or learning new skills as you are quick to master languages, techniques and remember new information. What's more, you can use this new information or these new skills effectively. You have confidence in yourself mentally and are realizing how intelligent you are. Many people do not excel at school, but later in life or in work it all clicks when you suddenly find something that interests you and which you are good at, and it is then you realize how bright you are – this is a year when you will gain far more confidence in your intellectual and thinking amiabilities. You can also rely on an innate wisdom and an ability to see the whole, not getting bogged down with unnecessary detail. In 2015, you could be called to write or speak in public, and you will uncover hidden talents within these activities that you never knew you had.

2015 is not a time to merely absorb what you hear, you are in need of truth and will only value information which furthers this quest – you will be critical of what you learn and choosy about what you elect to believe. 2015 favors investigative journalists, lawyers and researchers who look beyond the obvious to reveal the crux of the matter.

You will have a finger in many pies this year, and while you will tend to scatter your energy rather than directing it to one specific goal, the goal itself is broadening of your friendship networks, your beliefs and your vision of life and so focusing on one goal exclusively would defeat that purpose.

Sagittarians are seekers of truth and purveyors of wisdom, and it is the journey that is always more important than the destination and that is what this year is, a journey into new avenues of thought: many events will lead to many journeys, and where they lead is not as important as what you learn.

A very friendly and sociable year in which you will enjoy working with both peers and your wider community in goals that can unite and transform. Your power to motivate and imbue others with positivity can be vital in all careers and walks of life. This is a very idealistic time in your life where you want to imagine the best about those around you and where you can envision positive outcomes and solutions to even vexing problems. You are a great person to be around this year as you make everything seem possible. You must curb the tendency to have your head way up in the clouds – the feel-good factor which helps you tackle problems with confidence can also be the same feel-good factor that blinds you to issues that perhaps warrant some urgent attention.

Developing more tolerance is essential in 2015 – it's not all about your ideas, your vision and your truth. Sometimes you can become so wrapped up in your own bubble of ideas, aims and goals that you can come across as belligerent and over-opinionated. Stop to listen, and remember that learning never stops, and since this year is all about learning, part of that is listening well and reacting to what you hear.

One drawback of your positivity this year is the inclination to exaggerate or perhaps take a sloppy, slapdash approach to work which you find frustrating or boring. Be warned that you cannot ignore all details not matter how irrelevant they may seem to your overall goal. You need to be more sensitive to the feelings and insecurities of others – people have their reasons and they may not even be good reasons but they are still THEIR reasons for doing what they do, and you need to respect those rather than riding roughshod over them.

Sagittarius are vivacious and outgoing and in new relationships are eager to share feelings and speak about emotions which can help new relationships get off the ground fast. Existing relationships will flow well due to your bonhomie and generous attitude – it is a year where you tend to laugh things off and forget things quickly. However, sometimes you may come across as careless and almost too flippant to a partner who craves more intensity and perhaps a little more seriousness in the relationship, this can cause conflict. Being blunt and calling things as you see them may be the logical thing to do; however, some partners may be too sensitive for your brand of openness and honesty and so for the sake of harmony you need to hold back a touch. Do not try to convert your partner to your way of thinking – yes, you are changing your thoughts and perhaps adopting new beliefs or values this year, but that is your journey, not theirs. Do not expect to drag everyone along with you on your quests – others around you may not be evolving as fast or far as you, and you need to be patient with them. Of course, it is disappointing when others are like a wet blanket, but your challenge this year is to stick to your course and stay strong in your head, never deterred by negativity or naysayers. Play the long game and remember that some journeys can be lonely.

Single Sagittarians are more likely to bond with new partners who share their beliefs and goals – it is not a case of opposites attract when it comes to morals, philosophy and religion. This does not preclude unusual relationships that are very possible if you click, philosophically speaking. Relationships with those who are culturally different or from a different country are very possible, and you may well meet up with a new partner via a university, college or publishing venture.

You have a strong need to seek the moral high ground in all matters, which can be a little trying. You may rebel against religion (for example) then suddenly use it to back up your arguments or as a shield to deflect criticism.

You will gain a great deal from the outdoors and may go on several camping, hiking and other adventurous trips. This is both a competitive and successful year for sporting pursuits, both team and individual. You will seek new boundaries to push and new limits to cross.

It is a year of espousing high moral ideals and values and trying to make the ideal possible; however, it is important for you to be consistent and to practice what you preach at all times. Live your values and by all means try and actualize your ideal, but the high standards you have set can be onerous as well as virtuous.

Freedom of thought and movement are important to you, and you will not be able to tolerate any kind of restriction easily. However, the planets are aligned to give you that scope you need right now to innovate and explore intellectually and practically. There will be positive surprises and flashes of inspiration that keep you going and keep you overcoming any obstacles.

You can implement change and live according to your desire for change and novelty due to your organizational ability and foresight. This is a very good year for progress in mechanical, engineering and technical fields. You can make an impact on the world in terms of humanitarian work that relies on technological advancement. The hardest part of this year for you is coping with teamwork; Sagittarius are team players by nature, but your general impatience and eagerness to follow impulses and pursue ideas can put you at odds with others. This year it is hard for you to cope with ignorance, intransigence and small-minded behavior as you are so committed to change and high ethical principles. The more you can have the freedom to work to your own routine and follow your heart the better as long as you can learn from and recognize you own mistakes – single-mindedness leading to a lack of perspective is often a problem.

While your idealism is your fuel this year, it can also cause you to deceive yourself about certain people or situations. Over-optimism can lead to disillusionment and must be guarded against, check yourself and look for errors rather than glossing over.

This is a very good year to use home remedies and homeopathic solutions to health problems. This is a year of excess and you are inclined to neglect your body and take it for granted – this is a year when you might pick up bad habits, i.e. smoking, drinking or perhaps experimenting with drugs, prescription or otherwise; do be careful of being lured into these vices and developing habits which are hard to break.

You can frustrate others by being non-committal and rather elusive – you can also develop significant blind spots to things you wish to ignore. You will get away with this in the short term, but realities will have to be faced at some point in the future.

An exciting year where you will often throw caution to the wind and act on impulse. You may pick up and go or simply tear up the script of your current life for something that promises more. You have much stamina and the physical discipline to carry through tasks; sometimes, however, the mental discipline is not there, and you may neglect details or rush from thing to thing in pursuit of the next best idea. You need to harness your energy and focus on what you are trying to achieve, you need to keep to your established goals, not neglecting the more mundane and practical elements of any venture in favour of your philosophical or intuitive perspectives on it. Even the best ideas must be worked through on a practical level at some point.

Sagittarians in full-time work may seek to change the way they work to provide them with more freedom in terms of time. You may take a sabbatical to study further. You may leave your current job to teach in the 3rd world for a year. You may decide to leave the job you do in order to teach others or lecture. You may well find a second income which involves teaching, writing or communicating – this may be a spin off from what you currently do. Sagittarians will seek to improve flexibility within their work, or they may seek more autonomy within their current work so that your fulfillment within your career is enhanced.

Sagittarians are seizing the day and taking advantage of a wave of enthusiasm and desire to pursue goals close to their heart to shake up their lives. Intuitive feelings, yearnings, a desire to learn more about life and to recharge your spiritual batteries will incline you to new hobbies, travel, new friends, new projects and new life journeys. Seeking meaning in everything you do, you seek to bring high moral and ethical standards to everything you are involved in. A year when your mistakes and successes are all intrinsically part of a wonderfully exciting and variety-filled year of quirks and surprises.

Complacency and the tendency to assume things is your biggest problem this January. You must carefully make lists and tick things off, try and be systematic and not haphazard about the way you go about things. Not thinking things through and being too hasty to act can lead to a dilemma later on. The thing is, you are changing your mind quite quickly and so what looked like a good idea two days ago may take on an entirely new perspective – it is thus not a good time for major decisions as information is coming at you from different angles and situations are in flux. You can be very sensitive to the opinions of others, and they may influence you in two ways: you may do the exact opposite of what they said just to show that you have a mind of your own, or you may be subconsciously influenced by what they have said, even if what they have said has no constructive value. Either way, their opinions may force you into acting when you should hold back and let things settle before you decide what to do.

The danger of this month is that you feel very objective, but you are actually acting according to what feels right on an emotional and personal level. You can always make the objective facts follow your own subjective narrative to convince yourself of what you are doing, but is that helpful in the long term? You may want to make choices that reflect how you have always done things, when perhaps now is a time to change old ways.

You will be challenged to own up to and begin to address prejudices and preconceived ideas when you are thrown into situations where moral judgment is tested.

Relationships with siblings can be up and down this month, and you will get the feeling that they are not really listening to you – it may be a sign that you have neglected your sibling relationships and need to spend more time cultivating them again.

January is set to be off to a flying start and your eagerness and enthusiasm to take up challenges is there. You must muster up some determination and staying power as when Mercury goes retrograde on the 22nd there will be pitfalls and problems getting your message across – this is why you must be methodical as any sloppiness of details will trip you up now.

LOVE

Intellectualizing emotions and trying to eliminate feelings from relationships can be the wrong way to improve communications. Emotions have a life of their own and cannot always be rationalized. Sagittarians are uncomfortable with excessive emotion this month, and that can lead to this over rationalizing and explaining way of feelings – it can indeed make you come across as a little unsympathetic. It may be better for you to chat about positive ways forward rather than trying to put a positive spin on negative things from the past. Some people like to lick wounds and sulk for a time, for them it is therapeutic and they move on afterwards; you should not try too hard to jolt your partner out of that habit or way of thinking in order to force your 'let's get on with it' method. Be more compassionate and patient in relationships and use your positivity to lighten the mood, not to lecture.

A good month to chat about your joint finances and how to spend or invest money, i.e., redecorating, home improvements, pensions or how you can save for special treats, i.e. holidays and new cars.

An excellent month for single Sag to meet new potential partners – you may flirt extensively and play the field as your options are many due to your carefree sparkle.

CAREER

A great month for learning new skills and meeting new people via your work. There should be quite a lot of work for January, which is great if you are having sales and promotions. Communication with clients and customers is vital, and you cannot lose any chance to put your name out there as competition is intense right now. If you work in a field which involves transport, distribution, travel, logistics or data flow, you must be well organized as Mercury retrograde can cause disruption in all these areas and so you are well advised to get ahead of schedule before the 22nd.

A very busy and interesting month for interpreters, teachers, copywriters and IT specialists: it feels good to be at work, and you are stimulated and highly productive – no black coffee needed. Sagittarians are very restless in January, and the more your work provides a chance to meet people, learn, challenge yourself mentally or travel, the happier and more fulfilled you are no matter what the workload. If you are not employed or are feeling that your work holds nothing that can broaden your horizons, this is the time for a CV sending out blitz – remember you are positivity personified this year and even gambles will pay off, so push the boat out and have a stab at some new career opportunities.

Sagittarians' problem-solving skills are excellent this month, you are mentally astute and keenly observant, as long as you think before you speak and are diplomatic when putting forward your solutions, you can make quite an impact. In business or employment, you can outthink and outwit your competitors, and you can do things fast.

LIFE

A busy and energetic time, when unlike last month you have the power and will to finish projects and get stuck right into the nitty gritty. It is also a month of brutal honesty, where you are striving to cut through niceties and get to the heart of any matter in order to deal with things and make things work better. You are very impatient and impulsive – it will be very hard for you to hold back this month and maybe that is a good thing – sometimes we need to just go for it, say it and do it.

Not the best month to work in teams as your pace and output will outstrip the others, and you may become frustrated at the progress. You will also not be able to handle indecisiveness and dilly dallying as you are keen to make tough choices and move things on.

You may surprise some this month with your unique way of tackling problems and getting things done. However, your ingenuity and unique approach is just what is needed. You can be rather obstinate, and if you feel trapped or boxed in you will lash out verbally. You are not in the frame of mind to be held back by anything which is limiting, be that a person, a tradition or an opinion.

This month you will also foster all that is original and progressive in others, i.e. as a teacher or mentor you may be the one to see talent or ability in someone conventional wisdom has perhaps disregarded. You are inspired by anything which offers a way forward as you are in such an open-minded period of your life – you will read extensively or scour the internet, especially in fields such as new age, alternate lifestyles and politics.

You may get started on home improvement projects: you will want to make your home more organized, more aesthetic and more conducive to entertaining. Your home is the hub for social and family events this month, and you may spend some money on entertaining.

This is a good time to invest in your property, and any DIY that you do should enhance value rather than be purely cosmetic or short-term.

LOVE

While this is not a touchy-feely kind of month, it is a very accepting and open-minded month when you are both going to give each other more freedom and more space, and the result is going to bring you closer. Mutual respect and trust are fundamental, and the more there is of both of these qualities the more you can experience love and harmony. While in other aspects of life you may force the issues, in love you just want to let your partner be and love him/her for what he/she is.

'In' is the new 'out' for you both, and cozy nights together at home or even quiet glasses of wine on a hot night in the garden (for those of you in the Southern hemisphere) are preferable to spending the romantic month of February rushing about on the town. While this is a month when you will entertain in your home, you will be equally glad when you kick the guests out and have the house to yourself to experience a romantic moment. In marriages, it is certainly a month where you will look back and reminisce about good times and how far you have come together.

Your sex life is awesome this month with a good combination of passion and novelty.

Single Sagittarians are very good at getting what they want this month and so if you have your eye on someone, you can certainly win them over for Valentine's Day.

CAREER

An excellent month for inventors and those Sagittarians who work in scientific or technical fields. The pace of change in your industry is fast, and you are at the forefront with ideas and encouragement for the team – you are leading from the front and driving everyone on.

It is a very good month for thinking outside of the box and for bravely drawing up plans that have never been tried before. You have the foresight to know that often a new approach is needed and you are that person who can make that novel approach work. You are very optimistic right now, and that is encouraging for everyone as you are not likely to let obstacles get you down.

While you can be a little hard to work with this month due to your haphazard approach and your unwillingness to listen to advice or caution, there is method to your madness and you are persevering enough to make things work.

If you work in politics or social reform, you can be a driving force for good this month with the mental ingenuity and courage of your convictions to push through changes and change attitudes. You have no shortage of willpower and ideas this month and yet sometimes a certain intellectual superiority complex can win you more enemies than friends. You can achieve much, and you can certainly make a difference wherever you work by being the one who sees something others have missed or the one who is on the side of progress, but you are bound to alienate some and must work harder to be more diplomatic.

You may step on some toes this month; maybe you'll even get a kick out of that, but try and keep everyone on board to make things run smoothly for everyone's sake.

While there is an aggressive side to this month, you can actually get what you want very cleverly if you channel that aggressiveness into being intellectually sharp and strategic.

LIFE

The focus is very much on the home: this may be the month you decide to move home, convert the loft, build a garage, an extension or even a pool. Your impetus to change your home could come from a few places, i.e. a new baby, a parent coming to live with you, a child coming back home after university or maybe you are changing a room into an office or workplace so that you can work from home. Family matters may be the driving force for you moving home as well. If you moved a long way away from home in order to get a job, you might begin to think about moving back to your hometown. It is certainly a month when your home will change to adapt to your changing needs. Improvements made last month may help you sell or may give you the drive to make the bigger changes now needed.

Family relationships will also demand your attention – these are mainly parental relationships. The way you relate to and communicate with your parents is very important right now – changes within your parents' lives may bring you closer to them or previously unknown information about your parents or your background may come to light. You can find the issues to do with your parents rather disconcerting in the short run; however, in the longer term you can grow from the changes that happen now and healing and new starts are possible.

More generally, emotional issues attached to your childhood may resurface and since you are in a very positive frame of mind where you tend to be forward looking, what a great time to re-address these issues and finally put them to bed. There are things we all suppress, and they often resurface in very negative ways; however, this month the things that resurface can be dealt with very positively and effectively, marking a new chapter.

LOVE

You are very vital and energetic this month, and this favours your sex life and love life. Lack of time, lack of motivation and lack of energy are big problems for love relationships as what we all need to do is pour ourselves into close unions to make them work. What is wonderful for Sagittarians right now is that you do have that extra oomph and spark to place the vibrancy and excitement back into relationships. This is an especially good month for relationships where there are children and where you both work – you will have more time and energy than usual to spend on each other and a can-do attitude will replace a more defeatist, gloomy outlook.

It is a positive month of doing things together, getting out and having fun as a family – a feel-good factor will imbue all that you do. You are less stressed and, therefore, feel healthier, you are more tolerant and easy-going, you have your priorities straight and a good perspective on life; you are far less likely to fuss about minor issues. Being your 100% laid back Sagittarian free-spirited lover of life, what a better frame of mind to be in to ensure all relationships both new and old go well.

Relationships with in-laws can be very good: smoother and more hassle-free than usual.

It is a very good month for long-distance relationships and ones where there are cultural and religious differences – compromises are easily reached, and you are both able to gain understanding from each other.

CAREER

A very good month for those studying at university or working in academia – you can take onboard a great deal of information and will achieve a lot as you feel stimulated by the relevance of what you are doing.

Success is highly probable in all business and financial matters as plans are coming together and things are falling into place.

Economic events and events in wider society will have an impact on the way in which you work and on your business, and you need to be highly adaptable – this suits Sagittarians down to the ground as change and variety are what you are in the mood for. Events this month at work should give you an opportunity for travel, meeting a diverse spectrum of people and getting the chance to learn completely new ideas. International trade and new markets are very much in focus and may provide opportunities. Reaching new markets via your advertising and promotional strategies is essential – find ways to cross language and cultural barriers to expand.

If you are in employment, take any opportunity offered to study or learn new skills, even if it's a subject you have no previous interest in, you may be surprised.

In all work be more aware of the law and how it affects what you do, also take note of new international trade agreements, green legislation, fair trade or environmental laws which are in the pipeline and may affect you or your business at some stage.

This is not a good time to invest in mining stocks, large property portfolios, antiques or property overseas. Small businesses must be very flexible at this time, and so it is not a good period for entering into onerous contracts or long-term employment contracts – take on temps rather.

LIFE

During this month, you may feel a touch insecure. It is a year where the pace is fast and the events are sometimes confusing; there is not always a lot of concrete data or solid information that you can fall back on. You must rely on your wits and trust your instincts. In your heart, you feel positive and buoyant and yet your head is sometimes a little bewildered and craving of more stability and consistency. Advice and past experiences may not be very useful in helping you make the decisions you need to make, either at work or personally; this year it's all new and you will have to navigate some unchartered territory, and while this can be very exciting, it can also be a challenge.

This year is certainly full of change and variety. What there is a lack of, however, is routine and routine no matter how much we hate it can be a vital structure for us, which can give us an emotional or psychological anchor. This year and this month especially, you may feel as if you are on a ship trying to get your sea legs; you may even feel a little 'rootless' i.e. you need to get back to your roots, but they are not there, and there does not seem to be much to fall back on.

Being self-reliant and going with the decisions you make without looking back and without self-criticism is vital – hold your breath, close your eyes and jump. While you should accept some constructive feedback this month, you must not take it personally, view it dispassionately and make use of it if you can. You are very sensitive right now, and certain criticism may feed into your self-doubts and insecurity – you must repel any feedback that is negative. Your overall outlook is very positive; however, emotionally you are adapting, and that is what is causing some of the doubts and worries.

LOVE

Sagittarians may be non-committal in new relationships as you are trying to find yourself – this can be frustrating for your new lover who will find it hard to read you and know how to please you.

Sagittarians are rather enigmatic in love relationships this April – internally you are feeling rather vague and disconnected and, as a result, you are giving out mixed signals that are very confusing. In fact, your internal state of confusion can be projected onto the relationship, creating misunderstandings and a mis-match of needs. You feel more vulnerable than usual and are craving closeness and yet you are acting almost flippant and even evasive. Your insecurity may make you withdraw, which can isolate you from what you really need, which is a strong partner to take you in hand and hold you tight and tell you everything is fine. This is a month when Sagittarians who have strong partners will draw from that strength and allay their self-doubts because of it, this will bring you both closer together and result in a wonderfully loving and sexually fulfilling month. If your partner is weak, this is a month when the relationship will struggle and where there can be arguments and silences. If your partner is a critical and bossy person, it can also be an awkward month for you.

CAREER

This can be a very successful and productive month for Sagittarians who use their hands in their work, i.e. artisans, physiotherapists, chiropractors, carpenters, jewelry makers, potters, etc. You are nimble and skilful and can make use of a more sensitive feel for your materials or the body. It is a good month for those of you involved in healthcare, pharmaceuticals and alternate health fields. You are more sensitive to feelings, touch and emotion, and this is helpful for diagnosis and psychological support to patients.

April is also a very important month for those of you who rely on inspiration for their job. You can draw on a rich emotional fabric this month as you are feeling your own deep-seated and often neglected emotions more deeply and what's more, you are able to give concrete expression to those feelings in words, art or music.

You may find yourself mothering someone at work, and while your positivity can provide great comfort to them, it could become awkward if you do not know where to draw a line, and they could become overly dependent on you.

April is also a very exciting month for those of you who work in conservation, especially sea life and also oceanographers. Sagittarians are known as adventurers, and this month nature is calling you – your affinity with nature will be tested in pursuits like sailing, climbing or flying (i.e. gliding, parachuting) where you are almost at one with the elements and must use you judgment and your innate oneness with nature to navigate and make decisions.

LIFE

This is the time to make an impression on others; it is also a very good time to make new starts or to change direction. Your health and vitality are good, and this is a great month to start a new diet or to try out new diets or new health kicks, i.e. smoothies, green smoothies, kicking carbs for a week, no alcohol this month, etc. You may not want to stick with any particular new diet or health and fitness regime you start now, but the important thing is for you to try out new lifestyles and see how they make you feel – in a few months you may decide to come back to one of them. Why it's important to try different diets or exercise regimes is that one may just be the solution to a health/physical issue you are having, and you can turn your life about by discovering it.

You are very spontaneous this month and may on impulse do something that will actually create an opportunity for you; something you would not have expected. Be observant this month and take note of what people say and the new people you meet as opportunities for both romance, business ventures, and new friends are everywhere.

This is a very positive month for those who need to make public appearances: you may have to give a talk, do an interview, a presentation or a performance; you can give a very good account of yourself, but that does not mean you can wing it, you must be well-prepared and have all bases covered.

Mercury goes retrograde on the 19th and so make sure you complete the bulk of work to do with communications and writing before then, do not leave yourself with deadlines for after that date as events in your life will be unpredictable, and you may not have as much time to complete admin tasks/assignments as you thought. Complete on important contracts before 19 May.

LOVE

This is a good month for love as you are self-assured and confident, and thus able to express yourself and your needs in a positive way. Hit problems on the head by speaking about anything that is niggling immediately and getting it out the way – but read the next paragraph first.

There is a slight inclination to make too much of insignificant things this month – get things into proportion, and if you do raise an issue, make sure that it is important to you rather than merely a minor passing irritation. You are not always seeing things for what they are in May, and you may also misconstrue something fairly innocuous – think first and then speak up.

Single Sagittarians must be cautious as someone who seems wonderful this month may not be all that. Your perceptions right now tend to swing from too positive to too negative and back again and so judgments on people and relationship issues right now are impaired.

Love relationships can be erratic partly due to your fluctuating perceptions, but also due to a general state of upheaval in your love life due to workload, business trips and hectic lifestyles. Communication can still be very good if you keep perspective. This is not a cozy romantic time, but there may be spontaneous sex.

CAREER

A very good time to be pioneering and to do something totally different – this may be a new role at work, a new way to advertise your business or market yourself. You may also try a new software that can speed up your work or a new technique. You are very enterprising and ready to seize opportunities; if you are interviewing for new jobs, then this is a wonderful time as you are coming across as confident and capable and can give a good account of yourself. If you are awaiting a job acceptance letter, or indeed any other important correspondence after the 19th of May, check the post carefully and follow up immediately if you do not receive it as postal and communication problems are common with Mercury retrograde.

This is not the best time for teamwork as you have a strong desire to lead and to follow through on your ideas. It will be an effort for you to accommodate other people's ideas, but you must try and come across as cooperative.

In business, take a closer look at anyone you deal with, i.e. partners or other close working relationships and make sure your assumptions about them are correct. What are you or they taking for granted about this relationship – how can a frank discussion iron this out? Fixing problems now can lead to stronger, more effective relationships; all said and done.

In work, good fences make good neighbours – know your boundaries and make sure others know theirs.

LIFE

You can be rather indecisive this month and may chop and change between ideas and plans, you are having a month of last minute dot com, with 11th hour changes of mind. It is actually a difficult month to make important decisions, and that is why you are procrastinating – the information is vague and unclear, and so it is hard to make a rational decision, no matter how you weigh up the pros and cons.

Your best friend may have very important advice for you this month – listen carefully to what he/she says as he/she may have an entirely different perspective.

You are very imaginative and creative right now, and music will play a very important part in your life. Dreams, déjà vu and sudden insights can leave you confused, and you will have to gather all your esoteric brainwaves to decipher the information. The universe often gives us clues and hints to help us make decisions; however, they are often very subtle and even vague, and one must either meditate or allow your intuition to speak to you to help you decipher. The clues and the answers to your questions are there; be alert to the signs and use your heart to interpret.

LOVE

A month of far more clarity and calm in relationships after last month's topsy-turvy concoction of frustration, irritation, impatience and hassle. You realize now that no one is to blame, and the mistakes and misunderstandings were small and easy to forget. Resolving differences and maintaining an even keel in your love relationship comes easy; in fact, there is even a deep understanding between you that has been blossomed. Common goals are important in relationships now and so is pursuing mutual interest. Working and playing together lead to excitement in the bedroom.

A strong desire to understand others and take their opinions into consideration will help both new and older relationships.

Single Sagittarians are spoilt for choice in love and may have love interests at work as well as within your social circle – you are playing the field right now and are not in the mood to commit to anything serious that will limit your freedom. This is the best way to go actually as this is not a good time to marry, move in with a partner or commit relationship-wise. If you are in a relationship, do not take it to the next level this month. If you are single, stay that way and keep it to dating.

CAREER

Not a great month for big financial decisions or major strategic decisions. At work keep it simple and keep your head down. It is not a great time to take risks or try anything outlandish. Details are important as is trust – be careful who you place your trust in at work or in business dealings.

Be very clear in all your communications and make an effort to be specific, even if you are pedantic as misunderstandings, mistakes and misinterpretations are likely right now.

Do not allow yourself to be talked into doing anything that does not feel or sound right – stick to your guns, say NO and mean NO. Do not go along with the crowd or become inured to behavior that is not right, even if others in the office or your industry are doing it.

LIFE

What you define as success and achievement is under review in your life – you may have valued money and reputation in the past, however, now it is very important to you what people think and how you can use your profile or position as a role model to influence others. You will seek a platform to let others know what you feel is important – you may use your Twitter or g+ account, or perhaps if you are a lecturer or have a position of authority in your community, you may use that to educate people on issues to do with health, welfare, political, human and animal rights issues.

This month it is very important how you manage your reputation, both private and personal – be careful what you put out there in social media as once out there it can come back to haunt you. If you are a role model, you must pay special attention to how you come across, and if the messages you are putting out are consistent – can you be accused of not practicing what you preach?

LOVE

Sexual desire is enhanced this month, and your libido is high. Your willfulness and desire to have it your own way is also greater than usual, and ego conflicts are possible as you are identifying closely with your ideas and values and wanting to defend them passionately. Passion is the key – you are both passionate in the bedroom and passionate about expressing your feelings; emotions are running high, and this can bring you closer and thrust you apart depending on your mood. It can be a month of drama in the relationship, but that drama can add spice to your love life.

There can be conflict in relationships about the joint finances and how to spend and save respectively – you are not likely to take orders from your partner and may just decide to conceal your spending.

Secrets are also something in the mix this month – secrets are a good thing in a relationship as they add to mystery, and they can help you maintain boundaries. The challenge this month is deciding what you should keep secret and what you should talk about. Some secrets are harder to keep and can damage the relationship if they get out no matter how innocent. If you have secrets, you must also allow your partner secrets too, and that is not always easy to handle – can you handle it?

Your spouse may be instrumental in helping you with your career.

CAREER

Issues to do with loans and taxes can drain your energy and take up your time this month. Get organized and get your tax paperwork in order – better to do it now and get it out of the way. Improve your filing systems as with tax not everything can be stored electronically, you need original copies – make sure everything is filed away and labelled systematically. If you are in employment, think more about your tax and perhaps get advice to see how you can make tax free savings or reduce your tax bill via pension payments – get more info and organize your money accordingly.

Manage your online profile and encourage clients to leave endorsements or reviews on LinkedIn and online forums. The reputation of you and your company is essential, and you want to ensure that when you are searched or googled people see the best of you – enhance your SEO and make sure you are listed on all the local business directories. Get new business cards and perhaps redo your logo/website to ensure you are giving out the right messages to attract the clients you are seeking.

This is a good month to deal with members of the opposite sex, especially if they are in a superior role to you, i.e. your boss.

This is a very good month for those taking professional exams; i.e. chartered accountant, surveyor, financial advisor, bar exams, etc.

LIFE

Pleasure is actually in the little things this month – you may have many big plans, but you may just find that the best times come out of unexpectedly good moments which take no planning and don't cost the earth. If you are on a budget, fear not as a fabulous family holiday can be had this year for a fraction of what a fancy, expensive holiday could cost. It's all about finding out what really counts and realizing that there are wonderful things to learn about and enjoy under your nose, which you may just be taking for granted.

You may find that you are putting a lot of energy into things that no longer matter to you – you will have to review your life and make adjustments for who you are now. You want the things you associate with to reflect who you are, and if certain people or groups have evolved in a different direction to you, maybe you should cut ties.

You started off the year with a vision and then things got confusing and you lost impetus. This is the time to get the ball rolling again, making changes and getting some momentum behind your goal plans. You can be very effective in inspiring people or galvanizing opinion and getting others to take action.

A very good time to travel either mentally or physically – you have a need to expose yourself to new and challenging ideas: this can mean travel or even experiencing different cultures closer to home.

LOVE

For single Sagittarians, love can blossom on holiday and again this month is favorable for long-distance relationships. Single Sagittarians will be attracted to new lovers who have an air of sophistication about them or who are well travelled or well read – you want to learn from your lover, and the more he/she can introduce you to new ideas, new places and new concepts, the more intriguing and fulfilling you will find the new relationship.

Space to grow and appreciation of differences is what really contributes to relationship growth and to excitement. This is not about gelling and becoming reflections of each other, it is about reveling in what is very different about you and how those differences make life both exciting and challenging.

This month also brings new luck in love for those in same sex, cross-cultural or in alternate relationships – this is a very good time to speak about your relationships to help reduce prejudices and ignorance. For all relationships, this is a good month to 'go public' i.e. announce engagements, send wedding invites or just tell the world about yourselves.

CAREER

This is a month for expansion and long-term goal setting in whatever career or field you are in – set your sights high, and assess what needs to be done to get there.

This is a very good period in which to settle legal disputes and to build new relationships with other businesses – outsourcing overseas or looking to suppliers overseas is an option.

Many Sagittarians work in the legal field, and this month marks the start of a very productive and successful period where you can increase your profile and gain clients who are exciting to work with and from whom you can learn a lot. There is a steep learning curve for all Sagittarians at work now, and you have to put extra effort in to increase your knowledge – you may go on a crash course or an intensive induction process.

This month bodes well for publishers and promoters, especially if your products or books are about self-improvement, philosophy, self-awareness, growth and travel. If you work in a field where you seek to advance and improve society, either by creating awareness or raising funds, you can be very successful.

This month can mark a changing of the guard for Sagittarians in family businesses – you may be about to take over or take a bigger role, with a new vision. A family member can be a powerful mentor who can help you get your first job or on the first rung of a profession or trade.

LIFE

Looking for support from friends may lead to you supporting them more than they support you. Do you know when sometimes you do someone a favor, and they actually think it was them that did you a favour? Well, that is just what can happen this month, and it can get very frustrating. It is better left as it is, explaining it and trying to iron out the misunderstanding could make things unpleasant. Do not be tempted to speak to other mutual friends about it, as gossip among friends is a problem this month that can lead to misconceptions and bad feelings. Remember hearsay is not allowed in court as it is unreliable, and you should not base any of your opinions on hearsay either as it is invariably inaccurate, exaggerated or comes with a big ulterior motive.

Look within for support before you look to your friends and peers for emotional or practical support – their advice may well be useless and even self-serving, and with a little quiet time alone you will figure out how to handle it perfectly yourself. The answers lie within, not without in September.

You have the feeling as if the brakes are off and you are coasting this month in terms of career, lifestyle, and in general. It is as if you are a runner and suddenly you have had a second wind in terms of the goals you have set yourself, you will feel re-inspired and invigorated.

There is a feel-good factor this month, which may encourage some excess spending or eating, and so do watch out for that. Keep your sugar and carb intake controlled – enjoy your food, but eat well at the same time.

LOVE

You can be very willful and dramatic in love; you may make too much of an issue in order to make a point or to show that you have taken a stand. However, you must ask yourself – are you guilty of double standards? Do you expect your partner to abide by your guidelines or else, when you are not that keen on any restrictions or limitations on your own behavior and freedom? It is possible that in close relationships and marriages you have slipped into a mindset where you can only see what affects you and you react to that strongly, but you have lost the ability to see things through your partner's eyes. Are you too wrapped up in your own perspectives, do you need to seek more balance in relationships?

You may be getting what you want in relationships, but are you getting what you need? Are you perhaps reacting out of fear because the trust element is not as strong as it should be? Have you unconsciously set a script that you expect your partner to follow? Take a step back and look at yourself, try hard to think about what your partner is saying and how he/she may be feeling. This can be a very good time for relationships if you are objective and take positive steps forward instead of just scoring points. It's about listening and assessing the cause and effect factor in your love life.

Single Sagittarians need to be more discriminating about their friends and social groups as perhaps they are the reason why you are not attracting the sort of potential partner who can fulfil your needs and grow close to you. You are judged by the company you keep.

CAREER

This is a wonderful month for progress and concrete results, you are able to harness a self-discipline that has eluded you most of the year, and you are also able to knuckle down and do long hours of detailed work. This is a key time for organization and keeping to routines. You really can achieve much this month as there is more structure to your life and more predictability.

September is also a very opportune time to begin a new diet or exercise routine, especially as being fitter could support you at work and help you to be more alert, less tired and more effective.

Self-motivation, focus and an ability to problem solve and put ideas into a workable format will aid Sagittarians in all careers.

Accountants, secretaries, PAs, small business owners, IT repair specialists and systems analysts will have a very successful month.

LIFE

You will want to spend your spare time getting involved – yes, you are gung ho about projects, parties, campaigns, money-raising efforts etc; if anyone asks for your help you will jump in with both feet. You are up for impossible challenges this month – if it is said it cannot be done, then you are even more interested in trying. You are willing to take a risk if there is a chance you can achieve something of importance. You can be both a motivating and also driving force behind others or as part of the team. Teamwork and being part of something bigger and something important is vital to you. October is a month where you are concerned with matters beyond your immediate concerns, i.e. issues to do with conservation, poverty, human rights, justice or fairness in society.

You can achieve a high degree of emotional satisfaction and also fulfilment by feeling you are contributing to something bigger than yourself, and you can gain emotionally by sharing that experience with new friends or bonding with current friends more strongly through this shared purpose.

Things will tend to flow again this month, and it is a good month for decisions about money, finances and future plans.

LOVE

A very sexy and passionate month. A love of life and emotional warmth along with feeling attractive and vital bode well for love matters.

The physical side of love is important right now, and you should find satisfaction – you are very affectionate and tactile. You are the main initiator in love and will be up for surprises, gifts and fun day outs. Your extra energy means you are eager to fulfil the needs of your partner in the bedroom, and you are also keen to improve your 'technique'.

A new baby may be around the corner. Children in general will play a very important role in your life, and your own children will need special encouragement and emotional support. They can also be a big source of pride, which can bring you and your partner even closer. Doing things with your children and enjoying family life is fulfilling and relaxing. You may feel the need to start a family or extend your family.

True love can blossom for single Sagittarians who are pro-active in love – you are all set to meet a new partner and are up for blind dates, speed dating or joining clubs to meet like-minded people. Meeting people via mutual friends on Facebook may lead to love, or you may reconnect with an old school friend to find love. Take things slowly and do not be over-eager.

CAREER

This month favours work that has to be accurate and systematic – you can combine speed with accuracy, which is great for those taking exams and for those who work with tight deadlines in high-pressure environments. This is also great for those involved with science, financial transactions and business organisation.

October favors artisans and those who work with their hands where dexterity is important, i.e. craftsmen, hairdressers, carpenters, make-up artists, surgeons, those who play instruments and sportspeople. This is also a very productive month for those who compose music.

Small business owners can increase their efficiency and client satisfaction this month – make a big effort to deliver quality and value, these are the keywords. Rearrange your diary and the way you work to make better use of your time. You can be more patient this month, and your concentration is excellent, which will allow you to make the most of every minute spent on the job.

Consistency and efficiency are more important than originality this month – get the job done, and then think about adding the icing on top, not the other way around.

LIFE

You may decide to implement some austerity in your own life – you are feeling very self-controlled and want to make cutbacks in eating, spending and general waste. You are on a money and time-saving drive, not just for the sake of it, but because you have certain aims in mind, and you need to be a lean, mean machine to achieve these.

It can be hard to deal with authority figures and bureaucracy this month – obstacles imposed by government or frustrating rules and regulations can be annoying and time-consuming. This month, you will have to toe the line and may not have as much freedom to act as you wish.

Your relationship with one of your parents may be strained – you may feel as if they do not understand you and cannot be responsive to your needs. You may have to bite your lip and sign inwardly while you act dutifully.

You are rather run down this month and must eat loads of fresh green and orange vegetables along with proteins and fibre. You may find yourself addicted to coffee, even if you are watching your sugar intake – dieting should mean eating sensibly, not eating less of the good stuff as well. As long as you eat everything in moderation and avoid fast food, you should be on the right track. Moderate exercise regularly is preferable to energy sapping hard training or extreme sports. Make sure you watch your calcium levels.

You are willing to cooperate with others and are enjoying teamwork more than individual endeavors.

LOVE

Your feelings are deep and intense this month, and your passionate reactions may often overwhelm you. You are very protective of your loved ones and may enter conflicts on behalf of your partner.

Honesty and loyalty are key issues for you, and any feeling that your partner is not being as honest or loyal as he/she should be will draw a fiery response from you. You are not to be crossed this month – you can react very powerfully to hurts. Loyalty to you would include taking your side in arguments or differences you have with others – you do not want your partner to be playing devil's advocate, you want his/her wholehearted support.

For you, love means putting your money where your mouth is – deeds and not words are what count, weasel words and poor excuses will make you very angry.

Single Sagittarians will be reticent in love: less gung-ho and more thoughtful. You are feeling more sensitive and have your guard up this month, which is why you will want to take more time over new relationships than usual. In newly formed relationships, you may want a cooling off period in order to rethink things – is it planning out as you thought? Is it going where you want it to go?

CAREER

Play your cards close to your chest in order to avoid open opposition – be coy and do not forewarn your competitors of what you are going to do if possible. You are very courageous this month, and it will enable you to make tough decisions and take on roles that will intimidate others; be it public speaking, demanding leadership roles or having to deliver difficult news to staff or clients. You can deal well with taboo subjects should they arise in the workplace.

Your courage should not merge into a do or die attitude of brinkmanship – examine your motivations and do not put yourself or your reputation on the line unless you are certain you have evaluated other options and the fallout. Do not do the right thing for the wrong reason or it will not have the desired outcome.

Your spiritual will may be at odds with your ego right now – if you go for a new job/role/career and do not get it, do not be disappointed as maybe it was not meant for you – perhaps you were subconsciously not as eager for this new position as you thought, or maybe there was a bigger plan, a plan you cannot see the outline of yet.

Insuring your business property against burglary and also taking steps to make sure your systems have checks and balances to prevent fraud and hacking of important and confidential info is vital this month.

LIFE

This is the time for a good rest and to relax – you really need a mental break over December to unwind as it has been a very busy and fast-paced year. While many businesses pick up pace over December meaning more not less work, if you can plan in advance, I would try and factor in some time off so you can have a breather at some point. Do not take on any ambitious party planning this December, leave that to your mom or your sister; go to their house and let them do all the work, you deserve a rest.

Even if you cannot slow down as such and put your feet up, it is important to do things that are recreational and relaxing, and which allow you to switch off. There is the temptation to down the alcohol this Christmas, be careful to do everything in moderation.

You are highly practically-minded right now and can get things done, you are looking to wrap up things for the year efficiently.

One drawback of this month is idealizing the past and comparing the present to the past in a way that unfairly casts the past in too positive a light and the present too critically. Do not try and recapture the past or recreate it by trying to repeat places/people/events – nothing is as good the second time around. Live for now and do not allow reminiscing to overshadow the joy of now.

LOVE

Family relationships and the mutual nurturing within the family circle are important right now. There is a strong emphasis on respect and on the simple things that really matter. Giving is important to you, and you are giving of yourself in relationships, which will help love to flow.

You really want to share yourself, and that means opening up about feelings, emotions and fears – you can show your vulnerable side, which is very attractive. There is this desire you have to let your guard down and to relax, especially when in the company of your loved ones. If you are feeling as if you cannot relax and cannot be yourself now, then perhaps it is indicative that you are not as comfortable with your partner/lover as you could be – ask yourself why you are holding back? What questions and worries do you have about the relationship? What could your partner do to allay these fears and worries? The overwhelming desire is to trust and to be open-hearted with those you love, and if you cannot, this means there are certainly things you have to address. You will need to be honest with yourself about what you feel needs to change in the relationship and how you can change it.

This December is a magical time for relationships that are solid and honest; you can enjoy all the pleasures of the season together, and your social life will be filled with good friends and quality get-togethers. In December, you will be with the people who mean the most to you and who have the most to contribute to your life; this is not a holiday season of trivial frivolity, it has a deeper context and meaning and will be remembered for a long time.

CAREER

There is a feel-good factor at work, and you can see the best side of even the people that usually annoy or frustrate you.

You will have to work hard to be efficient as machinery breakdown, logistical problems and even structural problems could affect your workplace. Be prepared is the motto and leave more time than you need for all deadlines and journeys.

You do can create organization out of chaos this month – you do have the clarity of mind and strength of character to make critical on-the-spot decisions.

If you work in public service, i.e. A&E, fire and rescue, the clergy, local politician, police, etc. you may have to give up your time over the holidays to help and support others. It can, however, be a very fulfilling period where your level of fulfilment, job satisfaction and the camaraderie you experience actually makes it a Christmas to remember.

December is a great time for bringing creative projects through to a success – you will be able to cope with the organizational and coordinating side of artistic projects effectively.

THANK YOU FOR BUYING THIS BOOK – BEST OF LUCK IN 2015.

CPSIA information can be obtained at www.ICGtesting.com
Printed in the USA
LVOW11s1450120115

422492LV00002B/340/P

9 781503 323926